Copyright © 1982
by
Marcus Books
195 Randolph Road
Toronto, Canada, M4G 3S6

All rights reserved.
No part of this book may be reproduced in
any form without the permission of the publishers.

First Printing December 1982

Cover by Art Gardner

Manufactured in Canada by Webcom Limited

Note: Standard Botanical texts do not classify any of the plants dealt with in this book as poisons or irritants. However, individual reactions to natural substances vary widely, and neither the author nor Marcus Books can be held responsible for any adverse reaction arising from the use, misuse or overuse of the plants described herein. Always test any new substance in small doses at first, to ensure that no ill effect will be experienced.

Contents

Introduction (M.B. Cooke)   iv
Prologue   1
Symbolic Clues   5
Methods of Application   8

The Flowers:
1. Goldenrod (third eye stimulation)   11
2. Toadflax (love and knowledge)   13
3. Wintercress (reproductive system)   15
4. Vervain (balancing lower chakras)   16
5. Chicory (spurring spiritual interests)   18
6. Clover (calming the astral body)   19
7. Fireweed (opens soul to higher input)   22
8. Bladderwort (helps poor memory)   23
9. Cinquefoil (connects inner and outer senses)   25
10. Sweet Clover (understanding with the heart)   27
11. Bluebells (making decisions)   28
12. Canada Thistle (enhances spiritual gifts)   30
13. Sow-Thistles (releasing bitterness)   32
14. Joe-Pye-Weed (relieves spiritual burdens)   34
15. Gerardia (banishes fear)   35
16. Yarrow (raises dreaming consciousness)   37
17. Horsetail (balancing mental, emot. & phys.)   38
18. St. Johnswort (joins chakras together)   39
19. Reed (stimulates aetheric body)   40
20. Hyssop (releases sexual fixations)   42
21. Birdfoot Trefoil (heightens energy)   44
22. Aster (unlocks buried emotion)   45
23. Daisy (opens wisdom chakra)   47
24. Black-Eyed-Susan (opens heart chakra)   48

Epilogue   50

Introduction
by M.B. Cooke

Wildflowers is a curious little collection of 'spiritual lore' relating to the spiritual uses of a number of widespread plants that are easily found and recognized in the wild. The idea for this booklet came to me during the summer of 1982, when I was vacationing in the Bruce peninsula with Christine and the family. The Bruce is well known for its abundance of wildflowers and the large number of species represented. By chance — or is anything really by chance? — I had brought with me an excellent book, "A Field Guide to Wildflowers of Northeastern and North-Central North America, by Peterson and McKenny (published by Houghton Mifflin Company, Boston). This charming guide, with its color plates and the excellent line drawings, makes flower identification not only easy but intriguing. Spurred on by some unconscious urge, I proceeded to teach myself to recognize some three dozen of the more common species of wildflowers native to that area. Then, about the middle of our stay, we conducted a session in which Hilarion offered some input with respect to the 'higher' properties of a number of the plants I had been studying. He pointed out that the *herbal* use of wild plants, as normally practiced, does not take into account the possibility that certain of the species, and especially their *flowers,* could have beneficial effects at levels other than the physical. All of the growing plants, he stated, have *something* to offer mankind — though not always at the physical level. Some can open the chakras, others can free the consciousness from bitterness and resentment; still others can coax one's attention from material to more spiritual interests. It would be useful, he suggested, to codify at least certain of the more spiritually helpful species in a small booklet, and to make this available to those who may find it of interest.

Since I had already done much of the preparatory work, the production of such a book did not seem overwhelmingly difficult. Christine and I began to assemble 'readings' on various species of wildflowers, and of these, we selected the ones which suggested essentially non-physical or spiritual effects.

Most of the material which follows will be self-explanatory, requiring no further input from me. However, I should mention one point not covered in Hilarion's prologue, relating to the teas that are made by pouring near-boiling water over flowers: there need be no concern about adding any sweetener to the water. The recommended sweetener is honey, however, since refined sugar is a denatured material and thus somewhat unbalanced in its vibration.

Many readers of this booklet will be familiar with the Hilarion series of books, and the source from which they are derived. As I have explained in the earlier books, Hilarion is a being or entity whom I am able to contact through the use of a yogic technique by which the conscious mind can be stilled, and then tuned to sources outside the self.

I can give no personal guarantee that all of these wildflowers will have the effects described. The most I can do is to assure readers that none of the flowers discussed here are poisonous. I personally ate whole most of the flowers covered, and drank teas made from the others. Some of the flowers taste somewhat bitter, but none caused any untoward reaction.

The book consists of three sections transmitted from Hilarion, followed by the individual flower entries. For each flower reading, at least one applicable species is illustrated. The ones to which the reading applies are described in non-scientific language precise enough to allow any budding botanist (no pun intended) to make a ready identification. In any event, many of the species covered here are well known to the public and easily picked out: Goldenrod, Chicory, Daisy, Black-Eyed Susan, and others. The transmissions from Hilarion are set in different type from the material describing the plant for identification purposes.

I wish to express here my special thanks to Art and Joyce for their help in making this booklet a reality. Without Art's lovely drawings and cover, and Joyce's nimble fingers, *Wildflowers* would never have reached the bookstores.

It is my hope that the material in this booklet will lead to research that can open us up, as a race, to the many wonderful interactions that were planned between man and the other life-forms on the planet. By recognizing and accepting the gifts of the little wildflowers, we can advance faster than before toward our spiritual goals. And in addition we can have the wonderful experience of touching the tiny beings whom I have come to think of as 'the little lights of God'.

Maurice B. Cooke
August 1982
Toronto, Canada

Prologue

When the earth was being prepared for the advent of man as a species, much thought was given to the nature of the interrelationship that the new life-form should have with other forms which had preceded him on the planet. It was part of the Great Plan that mankind should become, through the development of the conscious mind, the master of the earth realm insofar as the land regions were concerned. The oceans were to be left as they began — a vast space for the co-operative development of many aquatic life-streams, without any one form dominating the others. However, for man it was believed that, after much time spent in plumbing the depths of negativity and waywardness, he would at last rise to take his true place in the scheme of things. This role was to be that of steward or caretaker for the other, less rationally conscious forms. As such, man was expected to be able to influence the other life-streams in a positive manner, for when a less developed entity comes within the sphere of influence of one more advanced, and is treated with respect and love, both of the beings move ahead in spiritual terms, especially the one that was less advanced to begin with.

Man, then, was to be the spiritual caretaker of the earth garden, giving to the lesser life-forms that spiritual impetus which comes through being treated with respect and love by a more advanced species. This was to be man's gift to the other kingdoms that share the planet, for through his loving leadership it was thought that all would ultimately benefit.

But it would not have been just for the gift to pass in only one direction. It was desired that the other life-forms and kingdoms should also be capable of offering *specific* blessings and gifts to mankind. *In this there were to be no exceptions.* The latter is an important point to grasp, and bears some additional explanation.

Consider the plant or vegetable kingdom. Many species are used directly for man's food. That is their gift, and they need offer no other. Of course, some edible species do contain other factors having nothing to do with food, for example the corn silk produced by the corn plant. However, as a general rule, each species has one primary area of 'gift'.

Other plants offer physical materials which man can use for manufacturing purposes. Cotton and hemp are good examples of this category.

Then there are those species which are able to bring man some comfort in his physical body, when through his own actions he causes that vehicle to be out of balance, and thus diseased. Much of the lore found in herbal books pertains to the use of various species of plants and trees for the relief of physical disease symptoms, and in general this information has been correctly transmitted. It is not our purpose here to go over that ground again, but rather to add a new level of awareness to man's understanding of the plant kingdom which surrounds him.

Work along these lines has already been initiated on the earth plane, by the author Bach*. This gifted and compassionate soul set about to show his brothers how many of the flowers available in nature could be employed to provide help in cases of mental anguish, fear and other non-physical conditions. Some of the Flower Remedies also have a beneficial effect on the physical body, especially in those cases were some physical imbalance has resulted from mental or emotional lopsidedness.

Again we do not wish to go over ground that has already been covered. As with all of our books through this channel, it is wished to offer the seeds of *new* ideas

---

*I do not hesitate to recommend to all readers that they obtain and read the wonderful little book, *Heal Thyself*, by Bach. — M.B. Cooke.

— fresh information which man can, through experimentation and thought, gradually develop to form the basis of a new and more comprehensive teaching, thus building up a corpus of knowledge that can be drawn on by mankind in the New Age about to dawn.

For in truth, the race of man has not yet at its disposal the kind of teachings and understandings which it will need in the early part of the Golden Age that is soon to begin. It has been our purpose in these books to *initiate* the process of revelation for the New Age. As yet, we have not been able to fully transmit a philosophy which will allow man to grasp the true dimensions of his position within the created worlds. However, we are hopeful that this channel — and others which we have at our disposal — will remain open and receptive to the efforts we are making to enlighten our earthbound brethren, for through these telepathic transmissions, we believe it will be possible to pass all of the information that the race may need for the spiritual and technical progress which man must make in a relatively short time.

Our purpose in this small booklet is not merely to show how a number of the little wildflowers of man's environment can be used for spiritual and physical improvement, though that is an important part of the reason for this work. Beyond such specific information, we hope to implant the concept that the nature which surrounds man can help him not only in physical, emotional and mental ways, but in a *spiritual* way as well.

There are plants that can open the soul up to energies from yet higher realms; there are others which can stimulate the development of spiritual gifts; there are still others that can bring the chakras of the higher bodies into closer connection. Some species can turn the matter-bound soul upward to more spiritual concerns; others can rid the lower mind of thought-habits that interfere with the soul's growth toward perfection; and still others can lead one to a true understanding of reality — an understanding from the *heart*.

Wherever the tiny colored flowers beckon in the wild, know that there waits an entity which holds a precious gift for mankind. The *category* of the help that is offered does not matter. Each species hides a pearl beyond price: it is merely for man, through knowledge, to reach out and accept the gift that is offered. For through that offering, the hand of God reaches down to heal, comfort and enlighten His earth children.

May the peace and blessings of all the higher beings who care for humanity's struggle be with your forevermore.

OM MANI PADME HUM

Symbolic Clues

Before discussing the individual species and the gifts which they hold for mankind, it is appropriate to explain in general terms the best approach to understanding the use of plants for healing and spiritual purposes.

We will begin by showing that the root, stem and leaf of a plant have symbolic meanings or associations which provide a key to understanding their usefulness. Those who devised the scheme by which the plants help mankind wished to make sure that a ready grasp of the subject could be had by anyone, and therefore steps were taken to ensure that, given the proper symbolic explanation, any person could readily see how the various parts of a plant would act.

Consider this: man is a 'triangle' — he consists of a physical level, an emotional level, and a mental level. We are here referring to the make-up of his lower self, i.e. the earth personality. These three levels correspond to the physical, emotional and mental bodies, and are perfectly reflected in the root, the stem and the leaves of a plant. The root is under the ground, and thus under the physical earth. As such it represents that part of man which is most closely tied to the earth: his physical body. The stem, on the other hand, rises up from the root, and has the function of conveying liquid and building materials to the upper parts which are forming and growing. Being thus essentially a conduit for plant juices, the stem aquires a 'liquid' association — and it is well known esoterically that liquid (specifically water) is a symbol for the emotions. Hence, the stem pertains to the emotional or astral part of man. Finally, the leaves are active in receiving the sun's energy and interacting with the air. Through photosynthesis, carbon dioxide in the air is broken down, with the carbon becoming incorporated into the plant, and the oxygen being returned to the atmosphere. Air symbolizes the mind or mental body, from an esoteric point of view, and thus the leaf has the same association.

But there remains the flower of the plant. Now it should be self-evident that the flower of any plant represents that part of the plant 'entity' which is the sweetest and most beautiful. Indeed, when a plant entity prepares to put forth and form its flowers, it gathers all that which is the sweetest and most evolved within itself (from a spiritual point of view), and uses this to literally make the flower and the perfume which it gives off.

We remind the reader that nothing is by chance, and that all phenomena hide levels of meaning vastly beyond what the commonplace mind can conceive. All seekers will thus understand that the beauty and fragrance of a flower represents a high spiritual quality, and that the factors which form the flower are part of the entity which resides in it. To gaze at a flower, then, is to look directly at the manifestation of the most sublime part of the little spirit which it harbours.

We have explained the general symbolic scheme of correlation for the parts of a plant. It follows that, generally speaking, the factors in the root will have a direct chemical effect on the physical body, those in the stem will influence the astral or emotional part of man, and those in the leaves will affect the mental or aetheric vehicle. However, it must be borne in mind that many so-called physical ailments have emotional and/or mental causes. Thus it will often be appropriate to recommend the use of more than one part of a given plant. Indeed, many diseases are so complex in terms of their causes that several plants or herbs are often recommended to be taken together.

Beyond the physical, emotional and mental components of man is that of the spiritual. As we have explained in our books, the higher self or soul of man exists and has its being at a plane or level entirely apart from the earth realm. But this higher part of man, too, can be influenced and stimulated by the lowly plants with which man's natural environment is beautified. For the most part, it is the *flowers* of the wild plants which are to be used when the soul or spirit is to be helped, as these represent the highest and most 'spiritual' fraction of the little entities that live in the plants.

Methods of Application

In regard to the use of the wild plants, we can say that much is already known regarding the employment of the root, stem and leaf. Generally, these are prepared as a tea and drunk. In rarer instances, they are used externally, in the form of a compress or poultice. As to the flowers, Dr. Bach has taught the homeopathic preparation of the tinctures which can be stored almost indefinitely. In this work we would also include an additional method — one quite suited for storing the more spiritual factors in the flowers (and other parts) of wild plants.

The method we refer to involves the use of olive oil. It is generally not understood just how important a gift to mankind is represented by this liquid. Olive oil, in addition to being an excellent eating and cooking oil, has a quality which no other oil possesses: namely, the capability of receiving and storing astral, aetheric and spiritual substances which otherwise would disappear.

For example, when a flower is immersed in olive oil, the substances of a non-physical nature which it contains pass into the oil and remain there — trapped until they are released by the administration of *heat*. The heat can come from the human body, or it can be augmented by the use of infra-red light.

The soaking of the flowers in olive oil should extend over three days, with the oil in a light proof container. Then the flowers are removed and discarded, and the oil is maintained in the container, shielded from any light. (Light would act to release the locked-up substances from the oil.)

The usual way of passing these non-physical factors from the oil into the physical or other bodies is to place a quantity of the oil at a chakra location. The usual chakra utilized is the ajna or third eye location on the brow.

In the short essays that follow, we will mention this technique where appropriate.

We should point out, in connection with the flowers of wild plants, that usually the non-physical factors can also be obtained directly from the flower through either eating its petals or making a mild tea by pouring near-boiling water over the whole flower and letting it stand for a few moments. Generally, the water should not be boiling, since in many cases this will drive off some of the 'spiritual' substances. Of course, such direct use of wildflowers is possible only during their growing season. For other times of the year, the oil method can be used. Those who understand how to make a homeopathic tincture may prefer that method.

We pass now to a detailed discussion of a number of the more common wildflowers available in North America and other parts of the world.

1. Goldenrod
(Solidago altissima)

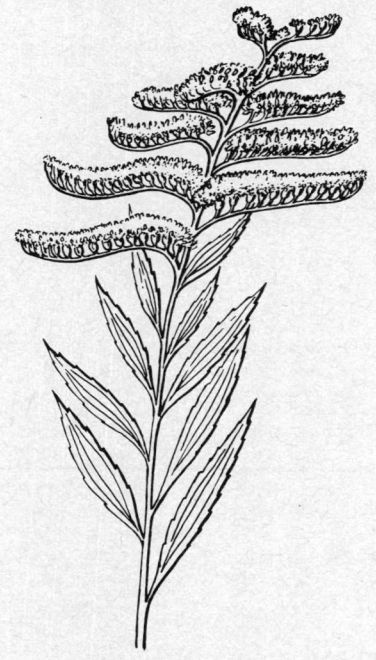

  Goldenrod is the common name for a large number of different species of the genus *Solidago*, and is characterized by showy clusters of tiny yellow-rayed blossoms massed together. Along with Ragweed, this plant causes much discomfort in sufferers of hayfever. The species shown is called Tall Goldenrod *(Solidago altissima)*, but it is emphasized that this is but one of more than 60 species in North America. The reading on this plant applies to all species of Goldenrod.

Commentary — by Hilarion
  "This plant has unfortunately earned itself a bad reputation, through its habit of profligately spreading its

fine pollen upon the late summer winds. We wish to prescribe an antidote for the respiratory problems that Goldenrod engenders, and also to disclose the primary gift which this plant has for man.

As with all irritating or noxious plants, the remedy can be found within the body of the plant itself. The hayfever syndrome which typically afflicts many who are sensitive to the fine pollen can be much relieved by administrating a tea made by boiling for two minutes the leaves and stem of the particular goldenrod which is responsible. If the culprit species cannot be singled out (as when a field contains a number of species), a tea can be made using all or most of the ones that are available. This tea should be drunk three times a day during the hayfever season.

The spiritual gift of the plant — and this extends to all species of Goldenrod — relates to an area symbolized by the very part of the body which is sensitive to the Goldenrod pollen: the nasal sinuses. These cavities in the head are connected to the ajna or third eye center, which lies on the forehead, between and just above the line of the eyebrows. They constitute a kind of resonant cavity which can amplify the pictures which the aetheric sight, acting through ajna, can pick up. By eating the flowers themselves, or by placing on the ajna a dab of oil in which the flowers have been soaked (see "Methods of Application"), an opening of the third eye can be promoted. With either of these methods the frequency is three times a day."

2. Butter-and-Eggs; Toadflax
(Linaria vulgaris)

   This member of the Snapdragon family has clublike spikes of snapdragonlike flowers with orange palates surrounded by yellow petals, and thin drooping spurs. The numerous leaves are narrow and the plant grows to from 1 - 3 feet. A courser species, *L. dalmatica*, has clasping oblong leaves. These species are found on roadsides, dry fields and waste places throughout most regions.

Commentary — by Hilarion
   "Here is a most fascinating member of the vegetable kingdom, for this plant has a double capability from a

spiritual point of view, symbolized by the two distinct colors which its flowers show: orange and yellow. Orange is the color of knighthood in the ranks of spiritual workers, for it denotes an ability to 'know' truth which goes beyond that commonly found. Yellow is the color of the sun, whose love for all creation is so vast as to be unimaginable by man — this being symbolized by the warmth and light which that mighty being floods out upon its surrounding space. Yellow is thus universal or Christ-love in action.

The combination of love and knowledge is a very potent one, and the seeker may move the more quickly in his chosen direction by adding to his other spiritual practices that of eating one of these flowers each day during the blossoming season. When the growing season has passed, the olive oil method can be applied. The flower-steeped oil should be dabbed on the ajna center and left for twenty minutes a day while the seeker lies still on his back. During this time all attention should be focused on the third eye location. Then the oil should be removed. After two weeks, gentle infra-red light can be directed at the ajna while the oil is in place, so that extra heating can be attained."

3. Winter Cress and Early Winter Cress
(Barbarea vulgaris and B. verna)

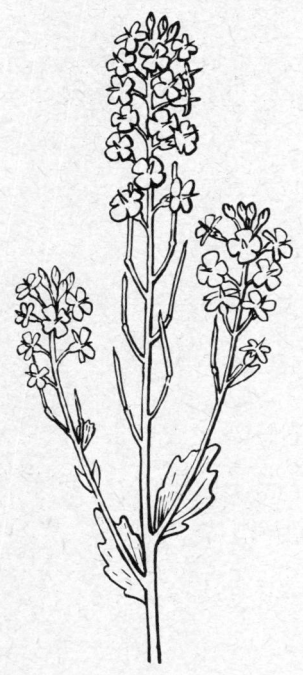

Note the small, yellow, four-petalled flowers in terminal clusters. Seedpods are erect, and longer in *B. verna* than in *B. vulgaris*. The lower leaves are shown separately in the illustration. Those of *B. verna* have more lobes. Found in fields, brooksides, wet meadows, *B. vulgaris* being more widespread.

Commentary — by Hilarion

"This plant has the ability to cure or relieve a number of minor illnesses and complaints pertaining to the reproductive system. A tea made by steeping the fresh flowers and leaves for ten minutes in hot water (not boiling) can greatly relieve menstrual cramps if taken three times a

day starting one week before the onset of the menses. The root can be chopped, stewed and eaten to reduce pressure on the fallopian tubes during pregnancy. The stem may be chopped and soaked in olive oil (see "Methods of Application") to yeild an oily rub for the genitals when inflamed due to chafing, etc."

4. Blue Vervain
(Verbena hastata)

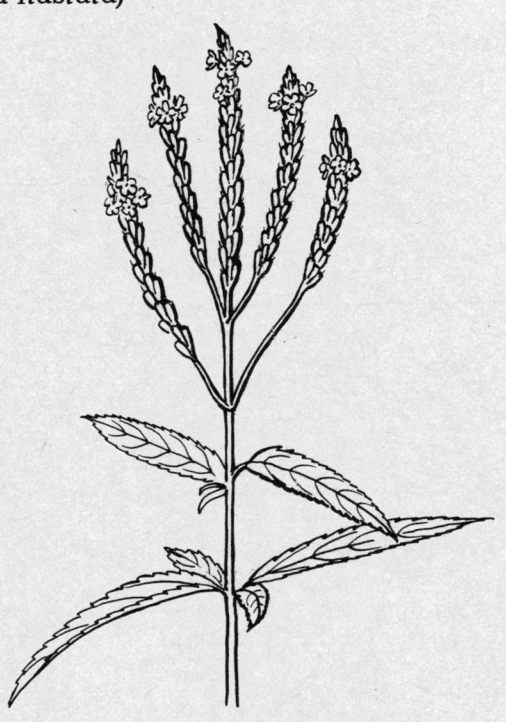

The widespread *Blue Vervain* is recognized by the branching, pencil-like spikes of small, blue-violet 5-petalled flowers which bloom a few at a time, progressing outwardly toward the pointed tip. The stem is four-sided, and grooved. The following reading applies to the other three commonly encountered species of Vervain as well though the effect is not as strong. These species are: *Hoary Vervain (V. stricta), Narrow-leaved Vervain (V. simplex)* and *European Vervain (V. officinalis)*. Only *Blue Vervain* is illustrated. Note that the flowers of *Hoary Vervain* are purplish rather than the blue-violet of *Blue Vervain*, and its almost stalkless leaves are hoary like the stems. *V. simplex* has narrow lanceolate leaves, tapering to a stalkless base. *V. officinalis* has flimsy spikes of lilac colored flowers and paired, deeply lobed lower leaves.

Commentary — by Hilarion

"This lovely plant is ideal for allowing the chakras of the lower body to become balanced. Many souls are in the grip of drives which stem from the over-stimulation of the solar plexus and root chakras, especially at the present time when energies of this nature are being shed by the earth entity in large quantities as she rids herself of the aetheric toxins which man has deposited in her.

The flower of any of the Vervain species may be washed, mashed into a gruel, warmed and eaten. It should not be boiled. The entire flower stalk should be eaten in this way — including the parts above and below the actual location of flowering. It is interesting that the flowers bloom progressively upwardly along the spike, for this sybolizes the 'raising' of vibrations which come about as the lower chakras are balanced."

5. Chicory
(Chicorium intybus)

This familiar and widespread plant will be readily recognized by many readers. The lovely, serene blue of the petals (sometimes white), with the flowers generally hugging the stems, sets this roadside plant apart from most others with which it appears. The rays (petals) are square-tipped and fringed, while the basal leaves are dandelionlike.

Well-known also is the use of the Chicory root for brewing a delicious natural drink. Many coffee substitutes employ chicory because of its characteristic flavor.

Commentary — by Hilarion

"The lovely pale blue flowers are a clue to the correct spiritual use of this ubiquitous plant. Blue is the color of

spirituality. A tea made from the flower petals only (see "Methods of Application") and taken twice a day for two weeks, can turn the interests of the lower personality away from the worldly and materialistic concerns and more toward matters of spiritual importance. The petals of the Chicory are so fragile that they begin to disintegrate soon after picking, releasing the non-physical materials that are stored. Therefore it is important to make the tea within 10 minutes of separating the flower from the living plant. The oil method can also be used, but again the flowers must go into the oil within 10 minutes of picking."

6. Red and White Clover
(Trifolium pratense and T. repens)

Both of these species have been illustrated, and the characteristic *chevron* on the leaves is clearly shown. In many areas, not all the leaves are marked in this way. In *White Clover*, the flowers and leaves grow on separate stalks from creeping runners. This is a familiar invader of lawns and grassy areas. Both are widespread.

Anecdote time. Back when this book was in the idea stage, and a few sample readings had been obtained, we were still not certain whether we would find the time, money and energy to produce it. I had already been given the clover reading, and thus knew the teaching regarding this plant. One evening Chris and I and my son Noel rode our bikes to a nearby park in Toronto, with baby Charles perched in his seat over my rear wheel. We sat down on a park bench and let the baby crawl off toward the concrete wading pool. My attention idly wandered to the grass at my feet, and I realized that it was rife with White Clover. Chevrons were everywhere. Reaching down directly under where I was sitting I plucked up the first clover leaf my hand touched. I looked, blinked, and looked again.

It had four leaves! The legendary four-leaf clover was staring up at me from my hand. Chris and I both burst out laughing, for we knew that the finding of this specimen was no accident.

"I think they're trying to tell us something," she chuckled.

"I guess we'd better do the Wildflowers book," I replied.

So we did.

Commentary — by Hilarion

"This flowering plant, which is so ubiquitous throughout North America, has qualities which are as yet unsuspected — even by experienced herbalists. It is generally regarded as unimportant aside from certain edible factors, but there is an important reason for the fact that it is so widespread — related to the great need presently for

the specific quality we have in mind. It is the quality of calming the astral body. The astral or emotional body, when unbalanced and agitated, leads to the distress and pressure which so may souls feel in their daily lives. Simply prepare a tea (see "Methods of Application") from those leaves which are strongly marked with the chevron. The more pronounced the chevron, the stronger the calming influence will be. The tea must be drunk just as the sun in setting for at least a week in succession, before the lovely calming effect will be clearly felt.

The directive to drink the infusion at sunset has nothing to do with 'magic', as some may think. Rather it is related to the fact that the energy rays from the sun and those from the earth are exactly at right angles to each other at sunset. At that time, an important calming effect can be obtained by anyone who is in a meditative or relaxed state of mind. That is why it is so soothing to sit and watch a sunset over a lake: the attention is directed out and away from the earth plane at the precise moment when the earth/sun energies form a right-angle. In a city, however, particularly amid the hubbub of a busy life, one rarely finds an opportunity to sit calmly for any reason. By drinking the tea made as directed above over a 10-minute period spanning the actual time of sunset,* the astral body can be more readily attuned to the purifying and uplifting energies then available.

It is important to bring this information about the clover plants to the attention of mankind."

*Most daily newspapers give the time of sunset.

7. Fireweed
(Epilobium angustifolium)

Named for its tendency to prefer ground that has recently been burned, this lovely pink-to-mauve flowering plant is readily identified by its showy spike of reddish seedpods angling upwardly, its four-petalled flowers above the seedpods, and the drooping flower buds above the ones in bloom. The leaves are alternate. It can attain heights of 6 - 7 feet and is widespread.

Commentary — by Hilarion

"This beautiful plant has the ability to connect the soul with yet higher levels. It is not of much use to the majority of souls now on the earth plane, but for seekers and those whose spiritual vibrations have already been raised through clean diet and meditation, a tea made from the whole blooming flowers (see "Method of Application") will produce energies in the lower bodies which open the

soul up to inputs from realms vastly beyond the soul's normal spheres. The oil method explained earlier can be used when the fresh flowers are not available."

8. Bladderwort
(Utricularia)

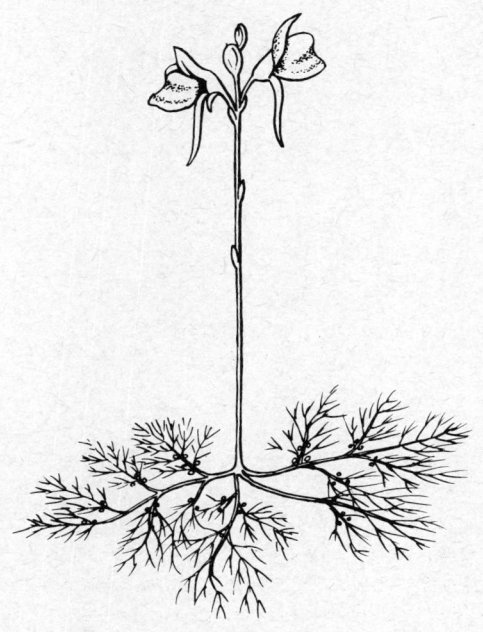

Illustrated is one of the dozen or more *Utricularia* species in North America. All have small yellow flowers suggestive of the snapdragonlike flowers of Butter-and-Eggs (q.v.). The flowering stalk is usually several inches tall and naked. Filamentlike leaves, usually adorned with tiny bladders, are submerged in mud or shallow water. The *Horned Bladderwort (U. cornuta)* has a drooping spur about 1/2 inch long. In the *Greater Bladderwort (U. vulgaris)* the spur is shorter than the lower lip and the filamentous leaves float horizontally below the water surface. The *Flat-leaved Bladderwort (U. intermedia)* has bladders on separate stalks from the leaves. The *Swollen Bladderwort (U. inflata)* is named for the swollen stalks of the leaves upon which it floats. The *Humped Bladderwort (U. gibba)* is a tiny plant (3 inches max.) with few filaments and bladders. Flowers 1/4 inch. The following reading applies to all of these species.

Commentary — by Hilarion

"A tea made from the flowers of any of the numerous Bladderwort *species in accordance with our earlier instructions can be very helpful in all cases of poor memory, mental confusion, and general exhaustion. The effect of the spiritual substances in the flowers is to unite all of the minds of the individual more strongly together: the lower mind (conscious and subconscious) and the higher mind. Instances of mental confusion and tiredness almost always arise from a poor connection between the various mental levels of the individual, and this charming little plant offers a wonderful gift for all who suffer in this way. There may be some cases of 'mental incompetence' or 'retardation' that can also be aided by this plant. The tea is to be drunk once daily before retiring.*

The key to determining the use of this flower lies in the bladders, since these were meant to symbolize the brain."

9. Cinquefoil
(Potentilla)

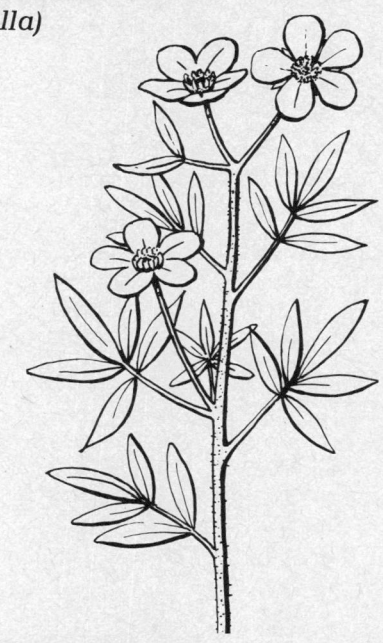

Many species of this yellow flowering plant exist. The reading below applies to only the three mentioned below, of which one — the Shrubby Cinquefoil — is illustrated. The name cinquefoil refers not to the five-petalled flowers, but to the five-segmented leaves. The *Common Cinquefoil (P. simplex)* has prostrate stems, rooting at the nodes. Flowers and leaves rise on separate stalks from runners. The *Dwarf Cinquefoil (P. canadensis)* is smaller than *P. simplex,* and the leaflets are more wedge-shaped, rounded, and without teeth below the middle. The stems are densely silver-hairy. The *Shrubby Cinquefoil (P. fruticosa)* has toothless leaf segments, and grows as a bushy shrub with larger flowers than the *Common Cinquefoil*. The leaves are silky and whitish underneath. The stems are woody, often with loose bark.

Commentary — by Hilarion

"These three species of Cinquefoil are able to bring into balance the inner senses and the outer senses. We mean, by inner senses, the inner ear and the inner eye. These are not to be confused with the organs of clairvoyant sight and hearing, which are seated elsewhere within the sheaths of the lower bodies. The inner senses — those which allow one to 'pick up' information, thoughts and mental images from higher planes — were always intended to be strongly tied to the physical senses, as indeed they were many thousands of years ago when man was more in touch with the higher realities. However, man's increasing materiality and his tendency to focus attention only on physical phenomena have led to an atrophying of the links that once united the higher and lower senses. The Cinquefoils named in the introduction to this message have the ability, when used to make a tea by steeping the flowers for 10 minutes in near-boiling water, to reestablish the connections that all men were intended to have as their birthright. The tea should be drunk twice a day. When the fresh flowers are not available, the oil method can be used."

10. White Sweet Clover *Melilot (Melilotus alba)*
Yellow Sweet Clover *(Melilotus officinalis)*

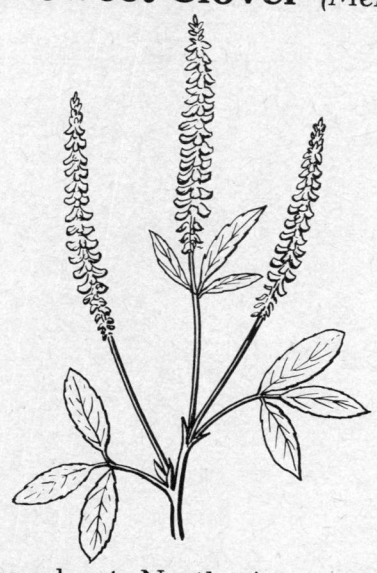

Found throughout North America, most parts of Canada and the U.S.A., this gangly, sparse plant with its slender, tapering clusters of yellow or white, clover-like flowers can grow to heights up to 8 feet.

Commentary — by Hilarion

"The major quality which is today lacking among mankind is the ability to 'understand with the heart'. This comprehension at the love-wisdom level would allow many souls who are now unable to grasp the significance of their lives to accept that all things have meaning, and that the events through which they pass are intended to broaden and render more spiritual the outlook which they bring to reality. The tiny flowers of these two species are able, when mashed into gruel and eaten cold, to promote an opening up of this well-spring of heart-centered wisdom, and to quicken that grasp of truth which is known by the heart alone."

11. Bluebells
(Campanula)

Two of the species of *Campanula* have spiritual qualities, and are those to which this reading refers. The two are *Harebell (Campanula rotundifolia)* and *Creeping Bellflower (C. rapunculoides)*. The *Harebell* has wiry, hairlike stems and linear leaves. Small rounded basal leaves wither early and are usually absent. The bells are violet-blue and nod from branch tips. The *Creeping Bellflower* has numerous violet-blue nodding bells mostly on one side of the stiff stem. Sepals are reflexed. Lower leaves tend to be heart shaped. Both species are widespread.

Commentary — by Hilarion
   "Many souls on the earth plane are plagued by indeci-

siveness. They are usually incapable of deciding personal issues when the choices are more or less equally attractive. Often this condition is represented astrologically by afflictions in Libra. One remedy for the condition, aside from serious effort of course, is to utilize the spiritual factors present in the two named species of Campanula. The shape of the flower represents the notion of seeing things clearly, for on the more subtle planes, the sound of a bell has the ability to clear away confusions, astral wastes and interfering elementals. Without these confusing factors, decisions can be made more easily. The method of use involves making a tea by pouring near-boiling water over three or four of the flowers, allowing this to steep for ten minutes, straining out the flowers, and drinking the water after it has cooled. When the fresh blooms are not available, the oil method using the ajna center (see "Methods of Application") can be employed. The frequency is two or three times per week."

12. Canada Thistle
(Cirsium arvense)

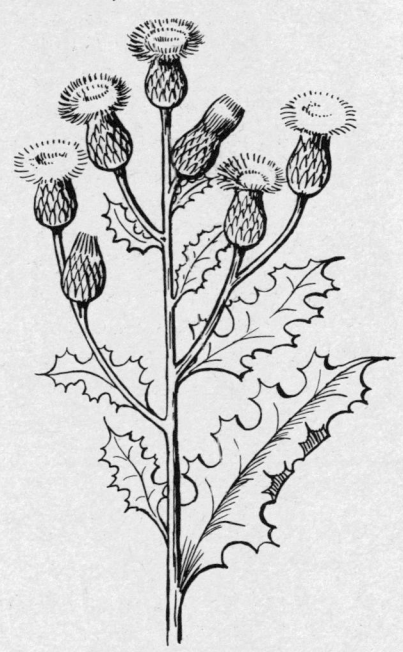

Known in Europe as Creeping Thistle, this is a hairless, much-branched plant springing from creeping roots. It has many small, fragrant flowers of pale lilac color, often clustered. Occasionally the flowers are white. The sepal-like bracts are pointed and often purple. It is very widespread.

Commentary — by Hilarion
"Here we have a most exceptional plant, for it has the capability of allowing those 'without' spiritual gifts to develop certain talents or abilities that might be regarded as parapsychological. However, the plant is non-specific in the help it gives, for it simply enhances the seed-gifts which are already present in everyone. On this point we

must explain that each person has some potential spiritual gift which, once developed, can be offered for the help of their brothers. It is simply a question of finding out what that gift is. For some it is in healing; others can channel music, art or poetry; still others have the potential gift of clairvoyance, clairaudience or prophecy. The main point is to accept the gift which manifests itself, and then seek to expand it. Do not hanker after gifts which you cannot readily develop, for there is a reason why they are withheld from you. Be thankful that God has chosen you to channel some of His wondrous energy, and look for ways to make that energy a blessing to your brothers.

This plant is used by making a tea from the blooming flower heads, including the bracts, which form a cup-like pod topped by the flower petals. Boil one half to one flower head in a cup of water for 4 minutes, then drink it just as soon as it is cool enough for the mouth. The boiling is necessary in this case to release the factors which must be put into the water. Each night for two months, take one cup of tea just before retiring, and during this period meditate on the matter of spiritual gifts. You will be clearly shown your own special area, and you will find your abilities in that area enhanced and quickened.

Some may find this tea quite potent. It may occasionally unsettle the aetheric body at first. However no adverse physical effects will result. In cases of such sensitivity, begin with a diluted tea — one part tea to four parts water. The strength can be gradually increased as the aetheric body becomes accustomed to the effect. The oil method is not suitable for this plant."

13. Sow-Thistles
(Sonchus)

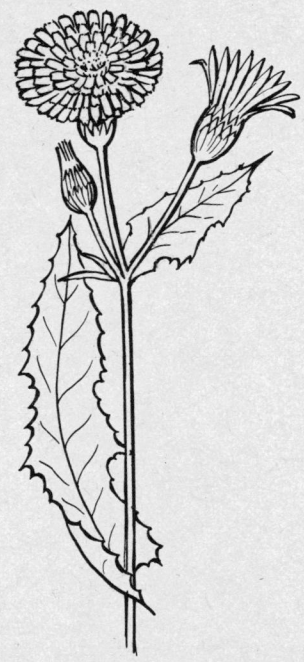

The *Field Sow-Thistle, Common Sow-Thistle* and *Spiny-Leaved Sow-Thistle (S. arvensis, S. oleraceus* and *S. asper)* are recognized by their prickly-edged leaves, their considerable height *(arvensis* and *oleraceus* to 8 ft., *asper* to 5 ft.) and the large, yellow, dandelionlike flowers. The following reading applies to all three *Sow-Thistles*, and variants or hybrids of the same.

Commentary by Hilarion
 "This stately plant has many noble qualities which it can offer to the human family. Among those of a more spiritual nature are the following.

 1. It can clear the heart of old hates and resentments. It allows one to release emotional negativity that has in-

vaded the astral body and tends to hang on. Of course, the person must want to be rid of the old bitterness or hatred, and must actively try to release it while taking advantage of the help of this beautiful plant. Simply eat the petals only of the flower (uncooked). They can be eaten alone or in salads etc. The key to this potent factor lies in the multiple rays of yellow petals. This symbolizes the multi-directionality of the purified heart — the one that can send love and affection out along many radiants at once, and so make of itself a 'miniature sun', reproducing at the human level the beating heart of the actual sun, which floods its love (in the form of light) upon all of creation.

2. This plant is also able to bring a calmness of the soul, especially for those whose recent lives have been filled with agitation or frustration. Such individuals often bring into this life a lopsided soul vibration which gives rise to friction with those around them. For help in connection with a problem of this kind, make a tea from the lower leaves — those closest to the root. This tea, made quite weak, should be drunk three times per day for a period of three months, during which the individual should practice deep, slow breathing techniques in order to induce a calmer spirit into his consciousness. Meditation should also be undertaken,"

14. Joe-Pye-Weed
(Eupatorium spp.)

The four commonly found species are *Sweet Joe-Pye-Weed (E. purpureum)*, *Spotted Joe-Pye-Weed (E. maculatum)*, *Hollow Joe-Pye-Weed (E. fistulosum)* and *Joe-Pye-Weed (E. dubium)*. In all of these, the dull, pale, pinkish-purple flowers are in a domed or flat-topped cluster. *E. maculatum* often has a deep purple stem, and all but *E. purpureum* can have purple-spotted stems. The leaves are usually in a whorl of from 3 to 5.

Commentary — by Hilarion
"This tall plant has the ability to take the mental and spiritual burdens from one's shoulders, by increasing an awareness of the oneness of all life and the Universal

Fatherhood of God. It may be consumed in the form of a tea made from the leaves closest to the flowers, with a small quantity of the opened flower buds also added. The leaves are the main ingredient, however. Do not boil. Frequency is once per day before retiring."

15. Gerardia
(Gerardia paupercula and G. purpurea)

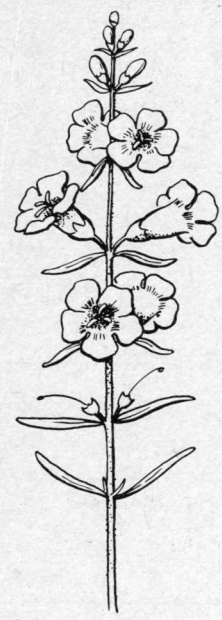

Gerardias are identified by the pinkish-purple paired flowers in the leaf axils, and the paired linear leaves. The Small-Flowered Gerardia is shown *(G. paupercula)* as it is the most potent of the Gerardias, but the reading below applies to the *Purple Gerardia (G. purpurea)* as well. Refer to any good Field Guide for identification of the other species.

Commentary — by Hilarion

"This pretty life-form has the capability of banishing fear and anxiety from the mind. It works on the astral body, and brings about changes which release the consciousness from the grip of fear. Any kind of worry or anxiety can be helped by this plant. Simply make a tea from the leaves and stem closest to the top, and drink this three times a week for an extended period. The flowers may also be used to relieve worry and fear, by soaking them in olive oil in darkness for three days. The flowers are then removed from the oil and the oil is retained in an light proof container. Application is by dabbing a small amount of the oil on the third eye location. In this way the aetheric flower qualities can be preserved indefinitely."

16. Yarrow
(achillea millefolium)

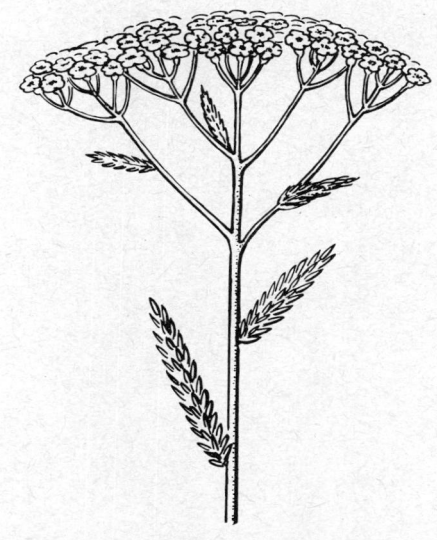

This plant has soft, aromatic, dissected, fernlike leaves and a flat, tight cluster of white (rarely pink) tiny, five-petalled flowers.

Commentary — by Hilarion

"Yarrow is a plant that is much needed by mankind at the present time, due to its ability to release the dreaming consciousness from the lower astral regions. Many souls are drawn to the lower astral in the dreaming state because of the coarse vibrations which surround them in their waking hours. The dream experiences in that region can be quite unsettling, even terrifying — particularly if the dream episodes are clearly recalled upon awaking. To use Yarrow, simply cut the head off and pour near-boiling water on it to make a tea. Let cool and then drink the water. This should be done just before retiring.

The same tea is also excellent for cleaning and stimulating the small intestine."

17. Horsetail
(Equisetum)

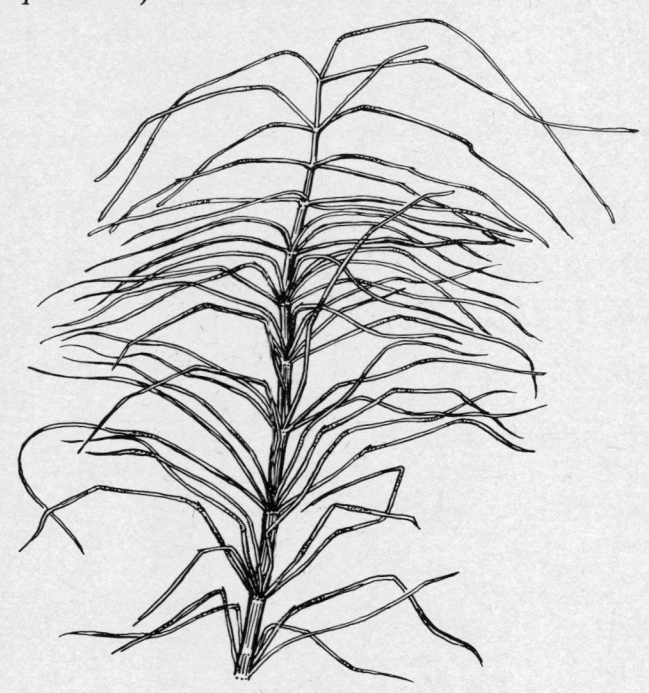

    This grassy, flowerless life-form is distinguished by the dark spots along the green, three-sided leaves, which branch out and curve upwardly from a central stalk. It prefers damp, sandy places, and is often found along creeks and in wet ground.

Commentary — by Hilarion
"This plant may be used externally as a poultice for bruises, contusions and other injuries where the skin is not broken. Boil the plant to make the poultice, which should include some of the plant itself, along with the water in which it was boiled.

    It can also be used for the spiritual purpose of balanc-

ing the mental, emotional and physical bodies. In this case, the poultice is placed warm over the third eye, while lying still on one's back."

18. Common St. Johnswort
(Hypericum perforatum)

This is the most commonly found of the numerous species of *St. Johnswort*, and is distinguished by the translucent dots on the leaves — clearly seen when the leaf is held up against the sky and viewed. The yellow, five-petalled flowers have quite bushy stamens. The following reading applies to this species and any variant or hybrid which has the translucent dots on the leaves.

Commentary — by Hilarion

"The dots mentioned in the foregoing description are meant to signify the many major and minor chakras of the body, and the ability of this plant, when taken as a tea made by pouring near-boiling water over several of the flowers only (steep 8 minutes), to knit together and balance the numerous chakras. The flowers may also be eaten whole, in which case only one per day is needed. The tea should be taken once a day, last thing at night. The oil treatment is of less value, as the spiritual factors of these flowers resist being leached into the oil."

19. Reed, Phragmites
(Phragmites communis)

This plant consists of a rootstock which yearly sends up a single shoot, to a height of between 6 and 10 feet. The stems are conspicuously jointed and hollow. The leaves are parallel-veined and can be as much as 2 feet long. The frond of seeds appears at the top in August. It is found throughout North America along ditches and near marshy, wet ground.

Commentary — by Hilarion

"This plant has an aetheric substance in the leaves which allows it to stimulate the aetheric body of humans, expecially in heated conditions, as are found in a sauna. When the human body is subjected to such high temperatures, the aetheric body expands, so that it extends up to 8 inches from the physical skin. In this condition, the contact between the plant leaves and the aetheric body is particularly cleansing and stimulating."

(This information came initially through Christine, my wife, when we were on a woodland walk. She was trying to 'see' in pictures what the various wild plants might be used for. When Chris received a picture of folks in a sauna, flailing each other with the leaves of this plant, she burst out laughing. Despite our skepticism, however, we did cut a number of samples, and took them back to the cottage for experimentation in my father's sauna. I can't begin to describe the sensation, especially when being tapped lightly along the spine. *The feeling was like water running down and along the arms — flowing out past the fingers. The energy vortex was incredible.* — M.B. Cooke)

20. Purple Giant Hyssop
(Agastache scrophulariaefolia)

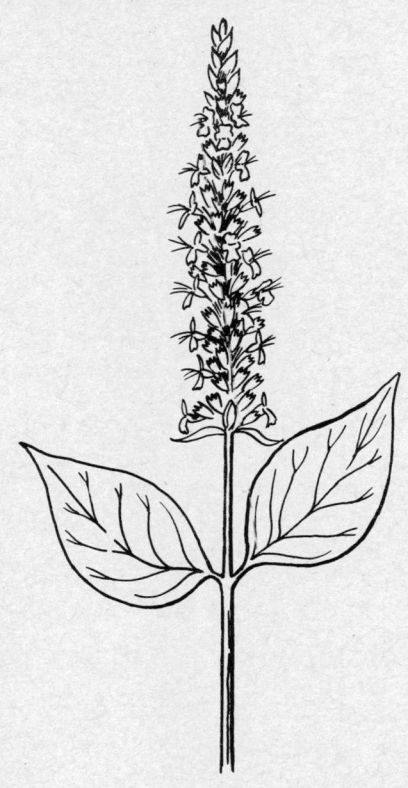

This plant grows to between 2 and 5 feet along ditches, wet woods and damp thickets. The flowers are small, lipped, purplish, and in a crowded spike mixed with purplish bracts. Four stamens protrude from each flower. Most leaves are coarsley toothed, well stalked, and white-hairy on the underside. The stems are purplish, with whitish hairs.

Commentary — by Hilarion
"The key to the spiritual use of this ubiquitous and

beautiful wild plant lies in the color of the flower. Few other blooms are so perfectly matched in color to the vibrational keynote of the new Age of Aquarius.

The flower itself is to be used, as with most plants that have higher or non-physical qualities. The blooming upper spike of the Hyssop can be cut just below the lowest flowering portion, baked in a 250°F oven to drive off all moisture and dry the flower, then mixed with pure olive oil and left to stand for three days. The oil is then ready to use. Placed on the third eye location of the forehead, between and slightly above the eyebrow line, it has an excellent ability to clear the lower mind of continuous sexual fixations, habits of lecherous thought, and tendencies to allow sexual pictures to obsess the thought patterns. Such thought-forms have no part in the coming New Age of love and light, and their energy must be transmuted upwardly to a more universal, caring form of affection and love, not only for the opposite sex, but for all members of the human family.

A similar though less potent effect can be had by boiling the flowers for 2 minutes to make a tea for internal consumption. This should be drunk three times a day. For the tea, cut the flowers from the main stem and use only the purple petals."

21. Birdfoot Trefoil
(Lotus corniculatus)

The leaves of this widespread small plant are in 5 parts — 3 cloverlike leaflets, and 2 more at the base. The flowers appear in clusters of 3 to 6, yellow to red. The slender lower pod of the flower suggests a bird's foot. Height is 6 to 24 inches.

Commentary — by Hilarion
"Of all the plants in this area, the little trefoil is the least understood in herbal terms. Its action is not at the physical but at the aetheric level. It is able, when taken internally as a tea made from the root and leaves (steep in near-boiling water 2 minutes), to open the aetheric body to energy inputs from higher levels, and to bring the energies of the aetheric, and thus the physical, into better balance. It is recommended for all cases of exhaustion, chronic tiredness, lack of 'spunk' or energy, apathy and

listlessness, and also nervousness and edginess. In the case of this plant, the most useful factors for combatting tiredness are not in the flower. What is in the flower is a wonderful capacity to overcome a tendency toward drunkenness and other forms of self-obliteration, for it can improve the self-image to the point where such blotting out of reality is no longer needed. The flower is used by making a tea in the previously recommended manner, and this should be drunk whenever the individual feels the urge to take alcohol or drugs. The use of the oil/ajna method is not effective, for the afflicted individual feels a need to actually drink something. Instead, the plant can be transplanted indoors, and 'tricked' into maintaining at least some blooms for most periods of the year."

22. Asters
(Aster spp.)

In the *composite* or *daisy* family, there are a great many species of the genus *aster*. All of the aster species show the effect described below to varying degrees, however the larger and more strikingly colored species tend to be more effective. One of the most showy and striking of the wild asters is the one shown here, the *New England Aster (Aster novae-angliae)*. The blooms are a deeper violet than the others, sometimes rose-colored. The leaves are crowded, toothless and lanceolate, closely clasping the stem, which is hairy. The flower has numerous petals, as many as 45 to 100. The floral bracts are sticky. This species grows to from 3 to 7 feet in meadows, wet locations and thickets.

Commentary — by Hilarion

"An important point to make about this and all deep violet flowers is that they match in color the basic tone of the New Age. As such, they can be counted on to be of particular help for those attempting to adjust themselves to the vibrational shift now occurring on the earth. Indeed, one could safely make a tea from any one or a mixture of basically violet-indigo flowers regardless of species, and be confident that the drinking of the tea would help him in his transition into the New Age. Of course, one should avoid the known toxic plants and those which produce symptoms that may not be desired (for example, Lobelia, parts of which are used herbally as a powerful emetic).

Especially in the case of this beautiful many-petalled plant, the beneficial effects are quite prominent. This and all asters can help unlock buried emotions from the past of the present life, and can also help to release blockages due to traumas occurring in past lives. During a two week period of drinking a tea made in the usual way from about half the petals in a single flower (twice a day — upon awaking and just before retiring) it is likely that one's emotionality level will be observed to rise, as many of the old buried emotional pains and traumas come up to the surface. If the emotionality begins to interfere with the normal smooth running of one's life pattern, the consumption of the tea should be reduced. The oil method can be used during the winter."

23. Ox-eyed Daisy
(Chrysanthemum leucanthemum)

This is the familiar and ubiquitous large white daisy, with the yellow disc which is depressed in the center. The flowers are about 2 inches across. The leaves are dark, narrow and many-lobed. It grows to from 1 to 3 feet in fields and along roads.

Commentary — by Hilarion
"This universal plant is one of the most important species which we wish to cover in this small booklet. It has the capability of opening up the wisdom chakra at the crown of the head, allowing a direct 'knowing' of

truth. The colors and the fact that it is so widespread are the clues to this quality. Often thought of as the 'humble' daisy, this little plant is in reality the queen of the wildflower kingdom. It is to be prized for the gift which it offers to each human soul. The plant is used in the normal way, making a tea by pouring near-boiling water on the petals only of one flower. Choose the most symmetrical and largest specimen that is available. Drink this tea three times a day. The oil/ajna method can be used when the flowers are not freshly available."

24. Black-eyed Susan
(Rudbeckia hirta)

This widely scattered and striking plant has a large, single, slender-stemmed blossom with numerous (10-20) long, daisylike rays and a chocolate-colored center disc. The leaves and stem are usually bristly, though some smooth variants are found.

Commentary — by Hilarion

"This plant, perhaps the most spiritual of all the species of wildflowers, is inhabited generally by a spiritual substance drawn not from the aura of this planet, but from that of the planet Venus. That planet is surrounded continually by the vibrations of Christ-Love, and therefore it will be understood that the tiny entity in each of these plants also partakes of the same purity and love. By drinking once daily a tea made by pouring near-boiling water over the petals only of one flower of a Black-eyed Susan, the heart chakra can be opened up immeasurably, and man can learn to love all the emanations and manifestations of the Godhead with the same universality that all of the higher beings can project. The oil/ajna method can be used as well, though many people would find the effect more pronounced by placing a dab of the oil on the heart chakra and directing mild infra-red heat at the same location. This should be done for only a short period at first — perhaps a few minutes — but this can slowly be lengthened to 15 minutes."

Epilogue
by Hilarion

The work of this channel has now shifted in an important sense. In our earlier books, we spent much time explaining the current phase of chaos and upheaval in the earth, showing that man himself had brought upon his own head the terrible times that are raging.

That phase is now over. No further warnings of impending disaster would serve any important use, for if man has not yet seen the folly of his materialistic and selfish ways, additional explanations are wasted.

Instead, we are now concentrating on providing, for those who are already attuning their vibrations to the New Age, a series of small booklets and guides which take up specific subjects and show how to integrate them into the philosophy of Love and Light for which the Age of Aquarius stands. *Body Signs* was the first such effort, followed now by *A New Heaven, A New Earth, Wildflowers and Vision.* Each of these books concentrates on one particular area, and brings to that area what spiritual perspective we may have from our level of awareness. It is to be stressed that these efforts are only a beginning. Many spiritual sources, acting through many earth channels, are required to transmit a fully rounded approach to reality — one which is consonant with the New Age of Light. But the work has begun, even as the spiritual vanguard of humanity has also begun to take up the mantle of leadership for the New Age. And here again we have the outworking of a great spiritual law: the Law of Response. According to this law, each time man takes a small step in the direction of spiritual improvement, the guides of the earth must respond in kind — by providing some extra help, input, explanation or whatever, that will help the process along even faster. The new books we have mentioned are thus a response to the great efforts made by the world's seekers to spread light and love among their brothers. It is the eternal cosmic dance: man takes a step — and the Brotherhood of Light responds. From another perspective, of course, the Brotherhood is merely acting out the will of the Father, and thus it can be truly said that each time humanity moves one step closer to its spiritual goal, the hand of God reaches down to add extra blessings and encouragement, so that progress can be even faster.

Indeed, the hand of God is never very far away from His earth children. Need one look any further than the beautiful little wildflowers which He has so profligately strewn at your feet? Remember that He smiles down always upon this tiny planet. Smiles and remembers ... when He walked and lived among you.

May the peace and blessing of all the higher beings who care for humanity's struggle be with you forevermore.

OM MANI PADME HUM

Lightline
A CHANNEL FOR ESOTERIC TRUTH AND INFORMATION

A bi-monthly newsletter allowing subscribers access to the Hilarion channel. General questions sent in are answered in this publication.

For more information write:

Lightline
　　195 Randolph Rd.
　　Toronto, Ontario
　　Canada, M4G 3S6